BURNING VILLAGE

BURNING VILLAGE

Menke Katz

THE SMITH
By arrangement with HORIZON PRESS

New York   1972

CONTENTS

CONTENTS

GOLD DIGGERS

Invitation

Stranger,
welcome to
our free inn with
four entrances like
the tent of Abraham.
Sweet cider sparkles for you
in cool, earthen jugs, our apple
trees invite all guests without bias.
Our mill operated by winds, prepares
bread from the field of peace. (Only cakes are baked
by angels.) Potatoes from our blessed underground,
water from our living well, birds may be caught if they
keep the salt put on their tails. A ride through a chat at our
table beats all the journeys, in and out of the nine planets.

Gold Diggers

Michalishek, village of my mighty
ancestors, bearded rivermen reared in woods,
with the chilled iron of axes in their glance,
foil the foe gnawing the root in its crib,
wean the saplings in their tree nurseries,
towing barges, drive onward to Eden:
Yiddish flowing as the Viliya river,
biting as the coarse teeth of a ripsaw.
Earthbred, illstarred gardeners with lucky spades,
digging potatoes like buried treasures,
gold diggers with potato forks ransack
the furrows stabbed with daggers of broken rock;
the potatoes — tricksters, play hide and coop,
in the tired earth of Lithuania.

A flock of roaming goats frolic around
the " hekdesh " where the beggars, the feeble,
the chronic derelicts loiter, grazing
the straw roofs blended with duff and leafmold,
hit by the evil eye of goat suckers;
the he-goats: whiskered, entranced goat-gods
gallop at midnight, in illuminous
ecstasy when terrorized by a falling
meteor, a mortal from Paradise,
a fugitive from the night sky, breaking
away from the chains of infinity,
bringing the twisted lanes into the
solar ranks as if dilapidated
Pig Street and the seventh heaven are one.

Eden on Fridays is always nearby.
Angels visit here like next door neighbors,
assert that Elijah is on the way,
with the Sabbath feast for the sabbathless poor.
Badane, mother of a craving fivesome,
depends neither on angels nor Elijah,

but on the miracle of her skilled hands
which pick the wood-sorrel, the berry-cone,
garlic, the pride of the lily family;
lentils, the value of Esau's birthright,
sauce sweetened and stewed to a goody pulp,
the keen aroma of cool ciderkin,
made of the tasty refuse of apples,
of rootstock, the seed, stem and skin of the grape.

If not challahs fit for a silver wedding,
a roll, by the grace of blessed candlelight,
with a scent of honey for the Sabbath queen.
If not gefilte fish stuffed with savored crust,
a herring, humble as fresh waters, spawning
in sod huts, legends of the North Atlantic.
Mead, (call it wine with a raw grain of salt)
served in laurel pink goblets from pitchers
born by the hands of village potters, with
ears and lips of clay licking yeast, honey malt,
adorned through ghost-fire in underglazed colors,
stored in dark cellars to drink lechaim
to each breath of every creature on earth,
at the light of the long zero winter.

Children in the rapture of reveries
see their father Heershe Dovid in far
America, mining the gold of the silks
fondled in the factories of New Jersey:
The " hekdesh " turns into a castle of gold.
Elchik leads the human wreckage into
a world baked like a round kugel, the moon
of yogurt, the stars — crisp potato balls.
Berke rides a bear made of prime confetti.
Menke sees Jonah in the kind whale, welcomed
with milk and honey. Yeiske is about
to reach the sun as a plum of bonbon.
Bloomke, the only sister, cries over
spilled milk of crushed almonds, to nurse her

pampered doll made of the sweets of marzipan.
O the dream is swifter than the wind, it brought
America into Michalishek.

Heaven on earth is in the children's eyes.
Who is richer in gold, America
or the sun? Elchik says: at dawn, the sun
is richer, at twilight, America.
Berke tells of a street — a dream in New York,
paved with silver dollars like little moons.
Menke in " heder " confides, his father
Heershe Dovid (tall, yearning and handsome)
sailed the seas to change his jaded horse
for a gallant filly, the squeaking wagon,
for a two-wheeled pleasure carriage; to trade
the cow with the drying udders, hardly
enough for milksnakes, — for a herd of an
aristocratic breed with teats like milkwells.
Sunset. Yeiske sees the clouds sail like boats
with gold which dad sent from America.
Bloomke fears there may be a shipwreck in
the clouds and flood the village with gold.

O the singing Jews of Michalishek:
O my unsung uncles, gloried horseshoers,
famed to shoe horses as they leap off the ground.
Jews with bodies like wrought metal; hammers
pride their hands over the anvils; felling
trees, hewing timber: robust, manful lovers,
lure the longing mermaids out of their streams,
to break their mirrors into dazzling charms,
to languish lovemad at their feet, to pine away,
on the mudlands of the Viliya river.

WHITE LITTLE GOAT

Old Lyre

Elchik plays the old lyre fit for king David,
handmade by the genius of a forefather.
The lyre has two open arms to embrace
the long forgotten world of its creator;
a spinebone which still has the tensile strength
to bear life many fabulous ages;
a brain made of the sensuous cells of
rare plants as wise as music, ears of seashells
reverberate the cry, longing and wonder
of marine animals. Only the heart
is invisible, hidden in every
tone picture. When he plays, it seems the soul
of his virtuoso forefather, petrified through
the lyre is telling of his life after death.

In late June as a farewell to Spring,
the wondrous lyre is hung on the roofcrest
so that the strings (made of gentle guts) may learn
the language taught by the wind, may allure
the melodies locked in the cobbled alleys.

White Little Goat

(New Chant Royal)

The house
is wondrous
as the woods where
it was born where trees
wounded by the axe cry
havoc, bleed like humans. The
earthen floor is scented with June,
recondite with the seven leaves of
the dogrose. Mother Badane hears the
brook rocking like a cradle, chanting of a
white little goat bringing raisins, almonds, good luck.

Here is
grandfather's
wainscot chair, the
panels sunk, the posts
turned, the carved white stork with
a child in its red beak, on
its way to a barren woman,
the wings chopped in flight, left whole is a
quill to write the grim fate of its voyage.
The effaced designs still show signs they were once
lordly oak, the hurt bark aches even after death.

Heershe =
Dovid, the
father lives in
a huge picture in
the brightest corner of
the shadowed house, enjoying
home ease under a lambent glass:
the flickering doubts of the twilights
and the distant fortunes of the good stars.
The light of the longing years are in his eyes,
his hands still wave good bye from the horse and buggy,

as he
started his
venture to the
never, neverland
America. The mother
Badane moves the heavy
picture from its snug shelter and
it falls leaving a gash in the wall
as deep as a grave, hurling the father
through a storm of corroded ages, glutted
with mildew-rot, through chips of glass, illfated as

broken
mirrors, stoned
by the wall which
survived the firebrat
(a host of moons ago)
who yelled: fire! — as he leveled
the village to the ground, called for
help the good devils who live in myths.
The father on the battered picture with
a cleaved skull, still smiling under dust,
time, ashes, as if he were buried merrily.

Envoy

The house on the bank of the river is like a
dreamboat, waiting here ages to tide across
the Viliya, to return to its trees,
to the nearby, dark forest. The winds
echo with the hopeful steps of
Messiah, calling the dead
to rise, to sail to the
Eden of Edens:
America!
Ha! A! Me!
Ri! Ca!

Aunt Beilke

I saw
my little
aunt Beilke as
a dwarf queen who fed
the village with wonder.
Her house humped as a weary
camel, a roof of reeds, straw, grain
stack; rushes bottomed the chairs, plaited
the mats, gave pith to the wicks, the rushlights.
Villagers closed their slop shops to listen to
the story spinner around the lone Sodom birch
which was known to devour unwelcome guest trees alive.
I saw gem-thieves invade the castles of enchanted brides
and vanish into the starless thieflands of her fairytales.

Rhymeless Triolet

My little aunt Beilke read
on God's palm the fate of man:
Not storks, crows carry children.
My little aunt Beilke read
the dreamtime of ages hence:
stars, beasts, birds, seas thirst for death.
My little aunt Beilke read
on God's palm the doom of man.

Toyland

Evening.
The children
see heaven as
a toyland where their
little aunt Beilke turns
the flaming sword which guards the
tree of life, as a merry-go-
round, she slinks through the eternal bars
of death to spin true fairytales again.
O she is wonder times wonder, her midget
jewelers (so tiny they stand in her ears) beat the
sun hollow to splendor the hovels of Pig Street. Night.
The children take a short cut through dreams, to America
where girls sleep in piebeds and boys suck boogymen of bonbon.

Rachel

Mother
Badane
milks the full teats
of her cow Rachel
with tuneful fingers as
a comely milkmaid (in the
half round seat of a three-legged
chair). Rachel, standing as a gracious
friend in time of need, her chin up, the end
of her tail — a love-lock, both cheeks of her fine
buttocks with blond dimples of light, still in early
bloom, pregnant with life, the mother of love, lambent at
the old day which dies through every crevice of the stable.
The children were about to send their big sister Rachel on
a caravan of clouds to America where rumors say,
cows give birth to gold calves, if not the
pestilence of fear in the village which seized even
Rachel who stands panic stricken, afraid to chew
the cud, her udders dry, her teats bruised, aching
with milkless fungi, she moos in terror
at the roar of any sexcrazed bull.
Mother Badane hears the knife
pray to its maker: condemn
me not to slaughter, let
me guillotine bread,
melons, apples,
the fruit of
Eden.

Cry Wizards

April.
All fools' month.
The palms fool the
palmreaders, the stars
fool the stargazers. The
village of Michalishek
echoes with the weeping of the
professional mourners, the elite
of the hekdesh, the beggar's guesthouse, the
womenfolk with eyes like unloaded tear bombs,
cry wizards who gathered to fight the oncoming
German armor with lament, bewailing yesterdays
todays and tomorrows dead, form a wailing chorus with
the homeless, the barefoot wanderers of Lithuania.

Witches' Sabbath

Amy the sorceress welcomes all witches to the orgies
of her Sabbath. Every shadow is a witch at midnight,
all winds are giggling fools, every dream, a tickling dunce.
Amy the sorceress leads the witches' choir: ha-
ha-ho, Germans here, not in one thousand years
and a rosetime. She calls her vampires out
of their graves (through spells and runes) to suck
to the last drop the blood of their
armies, the soldiers fall in
illustrious array, change
their skulls into crowns,
for her, the queen
of the nights'
witches.

TWO ARMIES

Before Battle

Listen to the silence, in the village
of Michalishek, a sudden voice is
like the crack of a whip. The ferry barge
rocks idly, yearns for its barefoot captain.

The houses huddle behind their shutters,
devour their sleep as a last meal. The night
is sawed into pieces by the crickets:
the fairy carpenters of the village.

Maidens hide in desolate attics, wreck
with their frightful steps the skilled labor of
industrious spiders who spun here through
dark ages their silk treasures undisturbed.

All around the muttering waters of
the Viliya river peel the bark of
the hewn trees; beyond, wild forests breed wolves,
local myths, haunted caves where robbers live.

Long winged petrels fly out of the burrows
of rocks to presage the approaching storms.
Jews at their midnight prayers hear the wind
saying kaddish through the autumn willows.

Two Armies

(Tanka)

Two armies — two foes,
two iron generals in
their panoplies of
fierce splendor, in their evil
magnificence, from soul to

sole made of medals:
the seals of death, outdazzle
each other across
the cascades of the two banks
of the river, dauntless as

their machine guns, two
gloried desperados of
kaiser, sword and czar.
Under their heels surge small fry
sergeants, mace bearers, cringing

hoards; gunbright soldiers,
wise as their guns, beam with right
and left shoulder arms,
with rifle salute, super
shockmen learn the miracles

of the gospels to
stride the waters like Jesus,
the prince of peace, drill
in reconnaissance, race to
thwart counter reconnaissance.

Snipers — camouflaged
dreadnaughts, concealed in ridges
hide in the hellmouths
of stone devils, under the
brute eaves of cliffs, prying through

snoopscopes into each
others sly schemes. A stray light,
weary as if it
traveled centuries, reveals
treasures buried in legends.

Dew on bloodweeds are
Job's tears, gems of misfortune.
A rosary of
a dead soldier's fingers points
to a gaping sky as if

it were guilty of
his death. A cliff resembles
a blind Samson hewn
of fog, cloudbursts, lightning storms,
groping out of the ages.

Time shackled his mouth,
stoned his scorn; rooted in rock
he is from head to
toes a tightlipped, clenched prayer,
to regain his ancient might,

to down from pillar
to post both horrormongers,
the valiant doomsmen,
winners of human carcass,
the purebred lovers of hate.

Both foes, impatient
as fire for the command to
draw the triggers, to
rush death out, to turn into
dung every likeness of God.

Both intermingle
their shout songs: rah!-rah! Hurrah!
hurray! huzzah! yell
themselves hoarse for each other's
throat. It seems barking barters

are here to compete
for their hellware, death is their
only buyer. The
riverway which transports the
timber of the wild forests

is a mirror of
cold steel: spears, foils, bayonets,
gleam in the hands of
terrorful cossacks bred on
the wrath of the fist, lulled by

the lullabies of
rattling musketry, suckled
from their mother's breast
lust for fire, swinging sabers,
whips, scimitars; saw their panes

clawed with frostwork of
bleak Siberia, winged with
caspian sea fiends;
taught by the sword and buckler
only the game of playing

havoc, of riding
bare horseback on the kill, quick
to reach the skull, the
true emblem of conquest, the
ghastly flag of victory.

Both armies pledge: not
a mouth of the enemy
will be left here with
enough breath to tell of the
grand holocaust. The Germans

howl: yah! the earth will
whoop and holler with cossacks

buried alive, the
Russians swear: we will build of
German heads a triumph arch!

Both armies — both foes
bear the same witness: death, both
are about to swarm
to doom to ash the comely
village of Michalishek.

After Battle

O the vicious calm!
Even the owl on the roof
is afraid to hoot,
listening to disaster:
the steps of night intruders.

Calm is the language
of stones on the only paved
alley — the warpath
of strangling armies through the
village of Michalishek.

Calm is the slumber
of unemployed plows, dreaming:
they cut, lift, turn the
soil, prepare the seedbeds in
deserted shops of blacksmiths.

Calm as the Godful
eyes of a lamb (a bleating
bundle of fear) which
plead for mercy under the
dazzling knife of the killer.

Calm is the tongue of
ghosts with long snouts and small tails
(of the slaughtered swine)
which haunt the forsaken barns,
smell the yellow blotches of

barley-scold, gnaw the
wheat and apple rot, leak the
milky stools stained with
the first milk of heifers, ride
on the skins of ponies, on

the yoke of oxen
who left here their sterile might,
their harnessed summers.
Calm is the wounded Saint Paul,
made by the saintmaker of

the village with a
heart of wax, eyes of fireclay,
a soul of melted
honeycomb, crying to the
cursed earth: O tomb of heaven!

Calm are the unmarked
graves of soldiers which keep rank:
loco and poke weeds,
corn cockle, the skunk cabbage
of starved Lithuania.

Hooded crows attack
the calm like carrion, crow
the names of unknown
soldiers, darken the twilight,
prophesy the end of days.

PRINCES OF PIG STREET

Gaunt Year

O the gaunt year of nineteen fifteen.
The retarded earth of Lithuania
smells with belladonna, mayapple, monkshood.
Smoke-beetles eat the soot of cold chimneys.
Sterile rains lament over the wasted fields.
Stagnant waters welcome the wigglers of
sociable mosquitoes, bosom friends of
malaria which sail in masses, floating
down the Viliya river on invisible
rafts to winter here, confident of
bringing chill and high fever to the village;
integrate, without bias, with the blood-cells
of birds, of young and old children of all creeds,
pledging allegiance to the flag of death.

Parasitic fungi own sick orchards.
The gall mites keep the blackberries redbellied.
Wingless larvae live in comfort in every
fruit, hatch from their eggs in the wine of the grape,
dine on love-apples, on bare twigs of the peach,
in early spring when it is still the flower
of promise, corrode the stone of the plum,
the grit of the pear, hollow the long, slender
runners of strawberry-plants, puncture the vine
of the honeysuckle. Scale insects burrow
in the bark, in the pith of the trees, bruise
the crown buds, strangle the roots, suck the nectar
of the lover Narcissus (until they remain
mouthless) leave only his reflection, longing
at twilight on every sash of the village.

Toadstools entertain dark elves in scrub-thickets,
like tiny ladies of pleasure under
mushroom umbrellas, until the hosts
poison their guests leaving only sunbeams,
dreaming of the tempting virtues of death.
The red haw, the black henbane celebrate
through night and daymares their venomous feasts.

Princes of Pig Street

September is as rich as King Midas.
The winds which shake the summer off a birch
remain with the curse of a golden touch;
as if the village cannot live without
the yearning of want it trades its prosperous
colors for the hue and clamor of the
moaning charlatans — the criers of autumn
which bring December in as a frozen ghoul.
Blackbirds cross the village to proclaim ill fate.
The owls in empty barns hoot disaster.
Mother Badane hears a suspicious rumor
in every breeze: Germans, Russians, both foes.
prowl through the forest of Zaborchi,
both victors count each other's carrions,
both fatten the naked heads of vultures.
Her lucky children, the princes of Pig Street:
Elchik, Berke, Menke, Bloomke, Yeiske,
still find crumbs of bread in the breadless basket,
their skullcaps adorned like crowns, in gaberdines,
woolen boots, winterbound, wealthy with the
dugout treasures of legends. Bloomke, their only
ever-blushing sister, her cheeks glowing
like apples of Sodom, kneads of the first snow
a laughing milkmaid, milking in two pails,
the snow like flakes of milk from the sky.

Still, as if some mystic command stopped every breath.
silence is a dumb, deaf and mute dragon.
Hush-sh-sh-sh, who is the strange horseman lurking
through the starry solitude of the village?
With one hand he guides his obedient
horse, with the other — the loaded carbine.
about to explode the calm of ages.
Each shadow resembles a Russian bear.
Vigilant: he is all-ear, all-eye.

Selah, the deadman's dog, believed to be
of the celestial hierarchy,
the friend of the dead, drowsing at the
crumbling gate of the ancient cemetery,
suddenly awakes barking at the intruder
all the curses of the valley of Hinnom
(which Amy the sorceress claims as her
private property). O who would dare to
penetrate here the eternal night,
if not Satan in his ecstasy of sin?

Beilichke, the legendary whore or saint
of the village, the walking doll of Pig Street,
lures the German armies away like Joan of Arc.
Her body is in itself a blond market.
She is from head to toes — vendable charm.
Her flirting arse is worth a loaf of bread,
an enchanted slop and a soldier's kiss.

Fire! Horses groan in burning stables.
A Bible burns in limbo like a
flying firebush, appealing to the merciful
and to the sons of the merciful.
In ashes of sepher-torahs sits Adonoi,
a black billet. Tongues of fire lick
a friendly wolf out of Isaiah's dream,
as it carries to safety a baby lamb.

A brave calf consoles a frightened lion:
" Brother, do not fear the angel of death.
We are all on our way to Paradise."
The little child leading us all since Adam
to the end of time, storms God off his throne:
Help O help, king of the universe,
but lo, God cries for help to the little child.

Jesus in a blazing church, horror-stricken,
seeking a savior through the savage heavens.
Itche, the convert, wearing one feminine

one masculine shoe, kicks the devil out
of the hallowed ashes of his fallen Lord:
No, not the lord fell, it is the fall of man
he sees baptized through fire, blood, dust.
He orders Yoorke the godsmith to weld
a new Jesus. He sees the souls of
the village hover in wind, hiding
in the fissures of uprooted tombstones,
in fear of Eden for even the Lord is on fire.
He hears heaven and earth, God's firstborn children
praying to Moloch for entrance to Gehenna.

Left of Pig Street is the wicked wonder
of flying roofs. The splintered houses form
ashen garlands, darken the light of
every prayer, remind there was once
a wistful alley there. The mudbank soiled
with bloodlust reminds there were once
people here. The shattered windows
saw thousands times thousands suns rise and fall here.

Yeiske

Yeiske, still a weanling, craving to be breastfed sucks apple
butter made of the sweet trash of goody cider, mumbles
in his crib, all delight: m-ma-me, heaven, give me
more heaven. He sees the speareyed generals, the
gilded brutes, true eyed boogymen who roam here
behind dying troops to goad battle cries
and listens to his giant brother
Elchik who leads his love Dveirke
through perilous stories, through
the terror of white and
red saviors: their
love oathbound, death
less, flare in
her eyes.

Menke

Menke, a child of
fear, his bare feet bruised by weeds
which fight stones, cleave rocks
for their lives, his tatters smell
of the tallgrass of the swamps.

Neverlands in his
eyes, famine in his teeth, shouts
for bread with a mouth
soiled with the waste of bleak fields,
as if out of a dungbath.

He muses over
a riddle: where is the most
wondrous puddle on
earth if not in this pot of
lentil soup — enchanted mud

simmering over
a deft fire, a flame of gold.
He hears the lentils
bubble, calling him into
choice tastes, only kings may scent.

Gripped by a trance, he
suddenly leaps into the
seething pot and turns
into a moaning puppy
smeared with fire, juice, blood: horror.

The wounds embrace him,
as if hugged by scorpions.
The lentils gloat at
him like eyes of sea monsters,
threaten to chew him alive.

Winter Soupbowls

O the soupbowls on
bleak souplines with a soupcon
of prehistoric

barley, fertile with
the germs of diarreah
(what an ideal

frolic for the gay
piggies of the village). The
bowls ornamented

by frostwork with all
fantastic foods, fit to serve
the king of vultures.

Noon. Dreams are guarded
by ice-locked angels, born by
the winter sunscolds.

Queen of Sabbath

Mother
Badane
welcomes the queen
of Sabbath with the
heavy sighs of oi and
vei, with a pot of morbid
odds and ends: wrinkled carrots with
the color of jaundice, lentils saved
from the mouths of snout weevils; the swollen
potatoes attacked by the late blight, plagued by
tumors, brag they are giant hills. A lonely bean
like a tiny kidney which left the waste in the pot,
a boiling hermit, plays solitude in the soupy seas,
circling, rambling, searching itself, squawking under the mist of
a yellow flame. " Lady," the cat with manners of the noble
hearted, born and bred on the hearthstone is here the sixth child
of the family tree. Her aged summers are wise-green
in her eyes, the color of thought is midnight on
her fur; her paws, medium gray, dimples of
grace, humor, pamper the five lank children.

— — — — — — — — — — — — —

Gloom of the dying lamplight. Lady
still meows kiddush to the ghost
of hunger. The guests: frightened
Sabbath-angels quit the
bleak house long before
the songs of praise
to them is
ended.

Little Brides

Little girls playing
brides are all out of cries for
their ailing snowmen:

O help us angel
of snowmen, the sun drinks our
bridegrooms, limb by limb.

O send us quickly
doctor frost before they melt
in the mouth of Spring.

The queen of spiders
who dolls her children in silk
gowns weaves with all her

eight fingers bridal
dresses for our wedding feast,
may she prosper here

in every nook and
corner a thousand winters
and a hundred Junes.

Little brides — little
widows wash with their tears the
windowpanes as their

snowmen rush home like
rivulets to their cloudlands,
to mother wonder.

Spring On Pig Street

Salamanders live
in fire, in the smoldering
ruins of Pig Street.

Old snows are young rills,
rushing, on their way home, to
return to the clouds.

Rains, tearblinded, strive
in vain to reach the nearby
Viliya river.

Memories at mid
night believe in the true moon
bows of April fool.

White ants, slaves, march to
celebrate the wedding flight
of their royalty.

Wool blinded sheep, clipped
by rainrot, remind of bare,
fate stricken sages.

Itching goats scratch their
fat scabs against the mourning,
charred walls of Pig Street.

The yearlings dance at
their first fleece round the regal
heads of proud thistles.

Twilight

Barges of ice float in the Viliya river, the winter
sails beyond the unknown. The sun, at dusk, is a Sabbath
kugel in a dream, last rays are envied by all who
crave to trade end for end. The puddle where piggies
wallowed the day away mirrors gold apples
which the children try to pluck until the
dragon who guards them swallows the whole
orchard in one gulp, then devours
himself, left in the mirror
is his tongue to lick the
fires off the window
panes and his claws
to seize the
first stars.

GENERAL HORSE

General Horse

1

Some say,
his evil
eye maims little
birds on their first flight.
Saliva drips from the
mouths of terror struck children.
His touch turns dew into spittle.
Firebeetles swarming the summer nights
like meteoric showers quench their strange
splendor. Even the unknown soldiers have no
rest in their graves in fear of dying again. In
intrepid visions he swallows the spears thrown at him
by cossacks, nimble as wild steppe cats on Russian steppes.
His voice echoes battle cries, only death cheers General Horse.

A nude
icon of
virgin Mary
is among the dolls
of his saint harem, in
his private olympus with
orders to scour his soul until
it is spotless as his armored boots,
multicolored as his mustache cup. His
thoughts are brushed to match the forelock, mane,
                    tail of
his mare, the halo of teutonic chivalry,
(taught to neigh in old, high German) whom he married for
the lure of her buttocks, polished as a wizard's mirrors,
a mare, jealous of his maiden goats, hogs and raped little girls.

3

Huzzah! General Horse (gammonfaced as if he grew on a
sausage tree) writes with his sword the farce of the century,
his muse is Shulamite, queen of the village, lovely
as the bride of the Song of Songs whom he ordered
to pick with her fingers as with dung-forks the
manure of his decorated mare as
he rides through the village crackling with
whip and spur; applauding himself
with his small, almighty hands,
as if a weird midget
condor fluttered in
delight over
carrion.
phoo! phew!

4

Against
the fires of
the village lives
on the scorn of the
beseiged Jews, in vanquished
axes, hoes, rocks; in pots, sticks
and pans. Their slapped faces hurt on
their trodden pictures which still smile, out
of their twisted frames, to the Messiah
of a future mankind, pray with ashed mouths: cry
God, at the work of your hands wherein you glory.
Is this man with the wondrous rib from which the mother
of life was born or a mare out of an incubus, a
thing worth a curse, a miscarriage out of the nit of a flea?

LAUGHING JACKASS

Laughing Jackass

Lucky the one who never heard
Bufo Bear — the laughing jackass
laugh. It seems, a thousand insane
asylums jeer at the fate of
man, worm and beast; pig, bird and mouse,
at the remorseless will of God.

O when Bufo Bear, the heavy
footed clodhopper laughs, he is
a swordless assassin loaded
with the mightiest weapon — fear.
It is said, toads of the family
Bufo leap in and out of the
pupils of his watery blue eyes.

Cronies whine like windbags as they
twirl with their thumbs the gossip
of the village. Whipcrackers in
the horsemarket run amok, crack
their whips over themselves. Specters chime
the bells of the forsaken church.

Rivers raid rivers, streams swallow streams.
Even owls shriek, pluck their plumage
with their strong talons and hooked beaks,
raise a feather dance in the wind.
Starnosed moles burrow beneath
the earth in fear of light.

Feeble wits in prayershawls
and phylacteries bless their
lucky stars, his laughter is
heard only at sunrise and
at the wistful close of day.

At moondown he stands in the
back of beyond — the fright and the

miracle of the village,
daring the armies of evil
to the final trial of combat.

His only ammunition is
a secret oath which keeps him
immune to bullets and a white
donkey which he found limping
through the crossfires of doomed armies,
defeating each other where all
roads lead to hell. O he can stand
safely against gunfire, and his
donkey braying fire and brimstone,
can bray down the might of any foe.

Verily, stunned cavalries in
battle array, galloping in
their three beat gait, flee in sudden
terror, raked by their own fire;
their riderless horses hoof the
dust of their trampled horsemen
when Bufo Bear hurls his laughter
rolling out like a thunderhead
of the pit of an inferno, —
and his donkey (waiting to ride
Messiah) in unison
braying — a frightful duet
of two wondermongers,
splitting the ears, cleaving the skull
and crossbones of the village,
announcing through a ram's horn
the arrival of Messiah;
the end of every hell on earth,
proclaiming the end of death,
the beginning of immortal life:

Rise O rise, dead of all centuries.
It is the end of graves, elegies,
coffins; death has been captured

or is in full flight. Death committed
suicide, drowned in the Viliya
river and turned into a live wave.
Our almshouse in heaven will be
a castle built of every star
of the milkway, every beggar —
a prince of paradise. Yea, death died.
Messiah is here! Me — ss! i — ah!

AMY THE SORCERESS
and
ITCHE THE CONVERT

Castle

The hekdesh — the village flophouse
is in love with blizzards for then
it is a castle flown by wind,
snow, hail, designed with choice gems, with
every known and unknown wonder.

Snow White finds refuge here with the
kind dwarfs, but may compete for her
prince, only among the wretched
sailor-poets who still sail the
boats sunk long ago, snore in their
dreams with sea-nymphs on diamond beds.

Brides sleep in the frostwork of the
castle, their lovers of ages
hence, are here to welcome them in the
winter twilight with the flowers
spun by the frost, with the wine of
red rubies, bloodstone, fire opal.

The panes are engraved with the rare
fruits, silks, gold of Ali Baba
and the forty thieves. The wind says:
Open Sesame and the chimney flies,
shut Sesame and the castle falls.

Amy The Sorceress

God's thoughts
are carved on
her healing rod.
Amulets of love,
said to be made of the
bark of the tree of life, grace
her ancient tatters. She dines with
the night crawlers on the rot of the
fields as they loosen the soil for the graves,
the gloryholes of the brave, the medaled, the
free. She moves with the rhythm of galleyworms as
they row the days with legs like oars. Skunk cabbage
                                smells with
Spring and blackleg, plagued by phobias;
perennial fear girdles the stems, obsessions crowd
                                the leaves.

Charmed Brook

Who stole the voice of the charmed brook which Amy the sorceress,
nursed in the mirrors of zodiacs, drunk with witches' milk,
nurtured in the solitude of the cosmos, in God's
loneliest island. Each drop like an earring of
a naiad, bereft of speech, the whole fairy
ring rolled out of the brook leaving only
dumb wonder. Left are seven winds to
tell the forgotten tales, to sow
memories of maidens in
love with ogres, their green
hair combed by elves, their
love guarded by
the bird: Feng
Huang.

Itche The Convert

It is
said, he eats
insane roots. O
he may outcraze a
whole insane asylum.
Moses is tattooed on his
forehead; Jesus is scarred on his
ghastly cheeks. In a rage he stones the
angels out of heaven, blinds God's eyes with the
dust of every new grave. At dusk, he is tarred,
feathered out of Pig Street as he gives the orders
of the night: " Witches, cast all your broomsticks to Jesus,
the Jew, the carpenter and God, to build a new ark for the
last flood on earth. Hail the king and deliverer of the Jews."

At The Pissbrook

A cloud
bathing in
a pissbrook is
a boat loaded with
dreams. Itche the convert
with a bold, red beard as a
blazing bush, with the airs of an
enchanted prince follows Amy the
sorceress through the illfated mirrors
of her evil eye, calling her, a conjured
lover, from the firecage of love: Come Bubo, my
eagle-owl, let us sail to the Land of Beaulah where
the river of death will lead us to life, to blizzards, the
rebellions of the gods banned from heaven as I from Pig Street.

Winter Dusk

Itche the convert
tells the day to fall, to draw
nearer a distant
dawn. Horns of ice gore God out
of the remorseless heavens.

Puddles are frozen
waterfalls, watermirrors,
through which Amy the
sorceress tells the fortunes
of stars, gnats, peoples, moons, mice.

Little girls — wood nymphs,
in the rapture of fancy
of the weird twilight,
create of snow a jolly
playmate: a new, wondrous Eve.

Selah

After Itche the convert fought
Jesus as well as Jehovah
for inviting death to lounge in
every eye of the gaunt village,
his only friend left in heaven
and on earth is Selah, the old
dog with occult eyes of a
cabalist, reared among the graves.

Hence, Selah is the chum of the
eternities. It is said he
learned Zohar, the redemption of
the soul, from dust. When Selah barks
through the fear-struck nights of Tishri,
his gratitude for being born
a dog instead of a human,
(the kith and kin of Lucifer)

then even the dogs awaiting
death in kennels know the days of
awe, Rosh Hashonah is here, join
Selah to bewail their fate, pre
ordained by the dog killer Pan
Hitsel, self-appointed angel
of death who caught them with bait of
a caress and guts of their kin.

Itche the convert and Selah
are verily one, together
they lead the wailing dog-chorus,
asking every dog: where is the
height over the highest height? Where
is the beginning and the end
of God? And the doomed dogs answer
hoo-how-l, hoo-hoo-oo, he-he-here.

Weary of howling to deaf gods,
the dogs see Pan Hitsel roaming
through their last sleep with an iron
gambrel (crooked as a dog's skinned
hind leg) digging a pit under
the lowest darkness of Sheol.
Autumn. Even the winds observe
Yom Truah, the feast of trumpets.

Dawn. Amy the sorceress feeds
her ghosts with the yolk of an owl's
egg. The mad juggler of the back
alleys juggles burning candles,
a candle dance: flame flowers to
amuse the souls of the dogs (which
Pan Hitsel flayed a sun ago)
gloried by the host of heaven.

Autumn

Itche the convert,
barred from God as well as from
the son of God, chased
by the star of David as
well as the cross of Pig Street;

he is free as an
autumn leaf, eager to run
from the commoners,
the laboring roots as well as
the pompous snobs — the crowns,

free from the good as
well as the evil. Even
in limbo is left
a friend — a self made noose, he
pampers in mutual love.

For incense he burns
the pink roots of onions and
garlic, the paupers
in the family of foods:
the balm and spice of the poor.

With the last light of
his eyes, he sees his soul mixed
with the ashes of
his Lord Jesus whom he saw
burn through the flames of Pig Street,

a torchbearer of
Eden and he heard Jesus
say: die, Itche, die!
No truth is as true as dust.
No love is as kind as death.

BREAD OF FAMINE

Bread Of Famine

(unrhymed, unrefrained, double chant royal)

1

The village is a bowl of droughts.
The creek is at rest in its grave.
Last drops of water still ooze like
tears from a weeping rock. The air
is crude with the odors of rich
weeds, of rough-hewn timber. Sterile
seedfalls breed a shriveled summer.
Horses, whipped beasts of burden, gaunt
as if skinned alive, neigh for their
burnt stalls, in mocked synagogues, leak
the oat-chaff out of their nose bags.

Mother Badane listens to
one grained wheat, the laughing stock of
the wind, praying for abundance
to the devil of dust on the
poor earth of Lithuania.
The barred garden ails through her
with pore fungi, early and late
potato murrain, blistered leaf
stalks of bean and celery blight.
The earth is overscented with
black horehound and red bearberries.

The children nibble the bitter
bread of famine: blue and green gall
apples, corky scabs left of the
potato race, vining squashes
of crookneck, of the fool's parsley,
tangled with bellyache, nausea;
they smell of crow and goosefoot, hedge
garlic, rose rust. The whiteblooded
mushrooms, hospitable witches
invite the parched village to drink
the pure venom from their death cups.

Sunset. Elchik sees a humane
spider, free of prey. He keeps watch
and ward as it weaves a net
of silk nerves on a gloaming pane,
entangling only the evening
star venus in its beautiful
cobweb. O a divine spider,
spinning each and every sign of
the Zohar, Messiah is on
the way to near the distances
of time, return to the first dawn.

This is why fowls flutter with drooped
wings and blue combs. Shorteared owls nest
in marshes. Strange birds with crimson
patches on their wings flap down on
the bombed almshouse. Menke listens
to the clock with its heavy weights,
counting moments as a miser
coins, dragging nights and days as on
crutches, O if he were a clock,
he would rush through all tomorrows,
in one minute reach Messiah.

Envoy

Arid Scrubland

Vines swoon with heat cankers in the
midst of their climb, cling to the loose
nails of the cemetery fence;
lilies with turk caps, violets
with teeth of dogs, strip their petals
commit self murder, welcome the
thorn gangs of the slum bushes. High
noon crowds the delirium of
schizophrenic beggars. Rootrot
shapes like diseased testicles. Foul
fruits are the Eden of vermin.

2

Berke, tall and lanky, ash gray.
It seems, the fires of Pig Street are
still smoldering in his eyes, the
hungriest of the children, sees
a mountain as a giant's bread.
Dusk is a sorcerer, turns the
house into a dwindling river
of honey, until a speck, a
leak, a promise is left. God's hand
drops the late sun to illumine
the beginning of beasts on earth.

He sees Adam yet void, hiding
from birth in the last bits of the
fifth day of life, cursing the dust
out of which he will be born. He
sees Eve weaving a garland out
of sow thistles which climb to grace
the outhouse, the oakmoss, the red
archangels soaked with the piss of
the ages. He hears Adam play

in the wind with fingers of grass
the doom of the first and last man.

Yeiske, the oldest baby of
the village with three sad autumns
musing in his eyes, years like late,
closed blossoms which fail to open;
still in his cradle, rocked to sleep
with mother's tearful hushabyes,
with a forehead like a sacred
parchment, ready for God to write
a Genesis without Adam
or Eve, without people, wars, graves,
crowbait or the hog cholera.

He rides on the old goat with the
dignity of a knight, beyond
the wooden Jesus where the wild
barley follows the trail left by
wolves and small red foxes, holding
on to the only horn of the
pitiful goat with a tail tired
of sweeping the larvae skippers,
its mouth grazed by awns and glumes, its
beard, a twisted scorn against God,
why it was not born a lion.

Bloomke in the deserted barn,
hugs a languishing harvest doll,
made of the last sheaf of summer,
with a head — a smart pumpkin, hands
and feet — stalks of wheat, with eyes, green
with envy of every living
child. One legged wine cups, limping
ghosts on canes, sated with dust of
bygone celebrations, still wait
for the vanished, laughing peasants.
Half moons remind of blessed sickles.

Double Envoy

A garden of fine needlework
fades on mother Badane's dress.
Crocheted sunflowers close their crowns,
laze their grace away like withered
spinsters, rosebuds yellow in Spring.
A child formed of a single thread,
interlocked with loped stitches dies
at birth in dry labor. Only
the autumn crocus is still in
bloom. Starved bees knitted with purl stitch
suck the nymph of a narcissus.

A peacock embroidered on her
blouse dies in ceremonial
attire. Two butterflies still play
love in the air as they mourn the
end of their lives at a bridal
wreath of white and black heart cherries,
thank the skill of her hands and the
needles which gave them a lucky
day, the darlings of the summer.
A titmouse, of bobbin lace, hides
from death in the hole of a tree.

CHILDREN OF PIG STREET

Summer

Breezes compete in
kindness to nurse the sores of
castrated steers, to
caress, mother the orphaned,
milk-ill lambs at their weaning.

Ivan the giant
boob who is said to move at
dawn a mountain to
a dale, return it at dusk
again, carries piggyback

his ever pregnant
sow and her herd of piggies
like muddy cherubs,
to the speechless rivulet,
to vacation in the lux

uries of bogmold,
piss, the lone-star-ticks, velvet
ants, buffalo gnats,
O all the stinkbugs, crushed by
the strong jaws of dragon flies.

O Ivan's piggies
the friends of the children of
Pig Street join in the
choir of singing insects, all
the droning, zooming singers

of the stagnant brooks:
soprano mosquitoes, loud
blowflies, bumblebees
out of their underground nests,
serenade Ivan's piggies.

Puddles gather here
to settle like little seas
where paper boats sail
through the skies to explore the
unexplored Americas.

Children Of Pig Street

Children with symptoms
of early blight, yearning to
break into bloom on
the tearful alleys of the
village of Michalishek,

bear on their faces
the puddles of the village,
the swamps of the low
lands, troublesome as the fire
weeds which thrive on the grief of

blackened fields, scorched by
the fleeing foes before the
wheat is bearded, run
the stray dogs away from their
catchers, the mice — from their traps;

climb trees to learn from
the loud voices of tree-toads:
(the weather prophets)
to predict rain, shrill with the
piping call of spring peepers.

Children — fugitives
hide with deserters of maimed
armies, in murky
haymows, in the ruins of
Pig Street, in bush and jungle.

Children — haunted by
the sister goddesses of
song and art, science
and music, adorn even
the outhouse with their fretwork.

They learn design from
frostwork on windowpanes, carve

hyenas with smiles
of hangmen on every sash
of the whitehearted jailer.

Butte, roof and mesa
is their stage, hurrahed by birds,
goats, brooks. Boys are Lenins,
Trotskys, little girls are red maids,
rouged with the blood of cherries,

imitate ramble
roses, cling in large clusters
on cemetery
fences, use the headstones as
barricades, in mock battles;

serenade the dead,
on whistling jars, teach parrots
to mimic the cry
and the laughter of the mutes;
hear lovebirds answer thousand

and one riddles which
the winds ask the graves since the
coquetting Eve lured
the handsome serpent in the
shade of the first apple tree.

Children, aerial
acrobats, perform feats on
trapezes, dance on
ropes with leg flings in Sophic
rhythms, buck and wing over

roofs like tigermoths,
announce penny rides to the
moon, play the snake and
the snake doctor, eat fire, drink
venom and piss blood; wistful,

see dusk in, dusk out
the sun — a fire chariot,
awaits Elijah,
to fly him to the heaven
of Sabbath and wonderfoods.

Mudman

Elijah is here,
disguised as a wandering
beggar, dragging the
mud of Lithuania
on his tatters. He comes at

dusk to show children:
death is a honey cherry,
the dying sun — an
apple of Eden. He points
to shadows growing through the

mirrors of twilight
like chocolate trees. He sends
doves through the fires of
battles, with lilacs, peace and
confetti under their wings.

He comes in nights of
Tammuz to change the arid
village into a
moonmad river of milk where
only angels come to drink.

He comes with the bread
which a preacher cast upon
the waters, brings the
almonds and raisins from the
songs which lull children to sleep.

He comes when Kislev
is sated with darkness, to
turn clouds into boats,
sailing to the land of gay
tomorrows: America.

Children leap into
dreams, to frenzies of delight,
spring into the air,
to reach the clouds, land on the
straw roofs, cheer themselves hoarse as

ravens, shout across
the seas, to daddy and to
America: ho!
we are coming, Elijah
is our captain — re-ra-ra,

enge-benge, stoo
pe-chenge, arche-barche,
gole-shvatze, ei
mele-reimele, bei-ge
le feigele, hop, hop-hop!

Mother Badane,
shushing the children mute, drives
them out of all their
deluded heavens: sh-sh!
Vei! good children learn from the

cobblestones to speak
the language of silence: sha!
The children, dumb with
grief, a handful of autumns,
little grandfolks, see the clouds:

Elijah's ferry
boats, transformed into dragons,
hear the rain drowning
America, hear the winds
splash mudfrogs at each other.

Piggybird

Menke, hungerworn,
gaunt as a tall weed, with a
mouth, acrid of goat
roots, rapebrooms, roams Pig Street from
dawn to dusk, shares his yearnful

childhood with little
pigs, his frolic elfkiddies,
his soul pals. Here is
Jolly Snooze with the voice of
a bass flute; there Bristlebird

with the small tail of
a rockwren. Here are Snowbush
and Blackgold, the twin
brothers, a mulatto dawn.
Menke, with the dream of a

flying little pig, flopping

his arms as in flight,
plays with the piggies — bird, yea,
he knows they are all
piggybirds, all little pigs,
all children, play birds, only

humans, the saints of
the vulgar play Satan. Who
if not he is the
troubadour of piggies? He
plays odes to their first summer

on his mandolin,
cut like a wooden pear of
a weeping oak, with
a neck, pampered by teeth and
nails of his toylike sister;

gorged with thorns, pebbles,
pens, by his little brothers.
The strings of a horse
tail speak the language which the
piggies understand: in love

with love, they hug each
other like little waves, rise
and fall, flow and ebb,
form a Springtide around the
sobbing mandolin, drum with

their feet a pixy
dance: squeal, crunch like ghosts gulping
a rain of lentil
soup, the Sabbath dish of the
village; their busy shadows

piggyback fields of
nonexistent potatoes,
change a shrew into
a hill of beans, carry a
slaveless world through safe dangers.

Evening. This he learned:
The day is kindest in its
old age approaching
late dusk. The wealthy sun dies
a pauper over a grave

of gold, donates all
its treasures for the little
pigs, on each dunghill,
through every pighutch. Menke
as if spun of the last rays,

is all light: Zohar.
O he outrays all twilights,

all galaxies. Night.
He sees darkness — black fire, the
brightest of all fires. His strength

startles even the
golem of Prague who stands here,
in his daydreams, a
humble brute, waiting to hear
God's name to give him life, to

avenge the cries of
the wretched. O all piggies,
all God's children are
sleeping beauties at midnight,
one wreath of races. They dream

their legs are wings, their
tails outwing cherubs in ease,
speed, grace. O they are
the envy of celestial
hosts, flying beyond the last

fall of man, back to
the starting point: the hopeful
void, the lowly small
voice of Genesis, guided
by the angel of first love.

Homeless Children

O homeless children
with the scorched look of burning
villages, in the giant

uniforms of dead
bolsheviks, like dusty toy
soldiers, rise against

God demanding life,
in the dumps of Pig Street. O
they scare the blues out

of the April skies,
loiter through twisted alleys
with the twilight bats.

O the waifs and strays,
closed buds growing underfoot,
folks rumor their cries

deafen the ears of
the scant breadgrains, darken the
translucent kernels

of the durum Spring-
wheat, leaving only in the
crippled fields — glume blotch.

Colonel Mendele
and
His Love Bloomele

" Colonel Mendele "
with the gay insignias
of brave corpses, lynx-

eyed with yellow ears,
strawberry tongue and cheeks with
a flare of famine

fever, commander
of Pig Street, bodyguard of
his love — Bloomele:

dimpled, fanciful
as if she canoed out of
his own fableland,

which she propelled with
her hands, as with weeny oars
to meet Mendele.

Her hair, hayscented
in five strands, braided in one
length, shimmering with

green and gold stripes of
empty sleeves with the rank of
garish generals,

iridescent as
the train of a peacock. His
rivals are: Velfke-

Zshoolik, toothy, sly,
gorging — a wolf; and Bentke
the wizard, sovereign of

the glitter of drowned
admirals, decorated
with all the stars, the

milkyway of the
onearmed, onefinned killerwhale:
Von Behr, still floating

with his sunk boat through
the full mouths of the river.
Mendele is hailed

by rhyming armies,
shout deaf the distance, silence
the winds: Salute! Ho!

Here comes our colonel
Mendele who shits love in
a gold fendele.

Feast

Children — comsomols,
pioneers, octobrists, wave
flags of the wretched,

see nearby the red
Messiah with a bread like
a dawn in his hands.

Children playing in
a Jack straw rebellion, mold
the old world into

a nile crocodile,
stuffed with dung, stab even the
rich sun with daggers.

Children, red princes
of death, live in forsaken
stables, barns, mangers,

charmers of the black
arts, alchemists build castles
of the pure gold of

manure, celebrate
the last days of their lives with
a rare feast of smells.

Their guests are harvest
mice who leave their nests (built in
the image of God's

globe) to join the click
beetles, the wireworms, the bot
larvae who prosper

in luxury, in
the itching nose of Yoodl
the coachman's horse, are

here to amuse the
sad dogs with dumb rabies, with
paralyzed jaws, throats.

" Cricket " — the bugler
promoted to sergeant cook,
has a finger in

every dungpie, in
each bonbon dropped by goats on
the lush floor of the

castle. Bentke, the
wizard leads all the pigheads
of Pig Street. O the

whole family of
suidae is here and their
kinship allied by

bloodbond, virtue or
affinity, all who find
here the smell superb.

Mother pigs enter
playing the bourgeoisie,
crowned with crow garlic,

grunt oink-oink like queens
in council, nonplussed which of
the delicacies

to honor first but
rush with undue haste to the
treasure quest of the

golden horse apples.
Father swine play feudal peers:
barons, earls, viscounts.

Bentke the wizard
orders his tin magicians
(whistling frogs, buzzards

loons, diving ospreys)
to croak abra cadabra
and pigs change into

princes, the princes
into worms: wingless cherubs,
crying for their wings.

Red Messiah drops
his fairy lamp, all new worlds
vanish, left are old

children wreathed with
roses of typhus fever,
left is the stupor

of delirium,
quenching the light of their eyes.
True is April fool.

NIGHT

Sorele

When Sorele the hermit was led out of self-confinement
to face the firing squad as a doomed bourgeois, she prayed:
O solitude O angel of the lonely, I swear
by the humble grass, by the infinite dust, I
am all yours, you are all mine, lovers of the
same undying night. — Cries, then, crouched, cramped, calm.
Only Amy the sorceress sent
and it grew into a beast-
and it grew into a beast —
god, barking: red! red! red!
death to any eye
which dares to see
white, pink, black;
red! red!

Night

Mother Badane
walks over ruins as through
a heap of bygones.

The moon parades in
full pomp a variety
show of joyous rats.

Brown, home-loving rats
rove through the feathers of torn
pillows; black rats nest

in trees; roofrats gnaw
the smokebeards of ghosts, born in
the chimney corners,

scratch the eyes out of
frightened cats, the leftovers
of vanished alleys.

A Feud, On Pig Street, Between Two Poet Friends

(twin sonnet)

1.

Oi, my
friend and my
enemy, if
worms can understand
my poems as you say,
then I am God-loved for I
am the friend of all cursed creatures.
O the worm is the victor of life,
stars, death. God is the father of the worm.
Your words smell of rubber roses: scare-flowers
where no bee may be lured to honeymoon, words which
give horsetails for forget-me-nots, gifts from lily-cheeked
Jezebel, nectar from royalhearted belladonnas,
bread for ghost towns: thorny manna raining from glass-eyed heavens.

Reply

2.

Come with
clenched fists, shout:
enemy! If
you see me as blue
beard then come stormlit, do
not tire my soul with the dull
hate of a sweet pepperbush, with
the sling of a stingless drone; such poise,
such perfumed spitfire outhorrors even
me: O comply with the wish of the doomed, bring
me for my last supper a stone from the valley
of evil, then leave in a laureled hood with the bells
of triumph chiming on as the musicmongers, the winds
accompany on my orphaned mandolin: amen, selah.

A Guest

A guest, a gay phantom, (scrawny as if he were skinned alive)
with eyes — beaming riddles, dancing among the wise fools of
Pig Street, beating with prayer sticks his organ beater.
Some see his arms like wings, an angel weary of
the heavens, celebrating his escape from
Eden. Some see him as a ghoul who steals
children out of dreams. Koo-Koo, the clown
pantomimes the guest in a dumb
show as a prince of eunuchs
who plays hymns to his lost
testicles, downed like
moons over the
Zenana
harems.

UNLUCKY STAR

Double Ballade of Queen Malkele
and Berele Bandoora

(unrhymed and unrefrained)

1

The almshouse gathers moss of the ages,
the scent of peat moor, of river bottoms,
briers, spines, prickles climb to the ceiling.
The hermit thrush builds here its nest, singing
of the yearning lovers of long ago
as if to remind the tired walls of their
proud descent of the woods of Zaborchi
where mother wolves suckle the stray children

from the dire lands of Lithuania.
The sky is kind enough to share its stars
with every crevice of the bleak almshouse.
Queen Malkele, the deaf-mute beggar girl
holds a cabbage as the globe of a new
planet, the purple leaves unfold in rare
rose cuts. Who is Queen Malkele? No one
knows which destiny conjured her here out

of nowhere: an awestricken riddle. It
is rumored she was born motherless on
the Viliya river, babied on wolf's
milk, reared on the blues of a tearful mer
maid, lulled by the hoot of an owl, grew on
the lucky bread cast upon the waters.
It is said, her ghastly grin may frighten
the bears out of the neighboring forests.

Envoy

Midnight. The skyful panes challenge the wise
light of the ancient oil lamp. Shadows sway
to and fro as mock pendulums, hoary

meteorites, in a sudden rush, whirl
out of the scorched wick, burning the wind which
wails in through the smoke-eaten chimney, still
belligerent, attacking death itself.

2

Now meet Berele Bandoora, the drum
beater, beating a thousand miaows a
minute with his musical fist, scares the
nine lives out of the alley cats. O he
is like the sun, a dwarf star, like the wind
a street musician. God bears witness, he
is the virtuoso lover of queen
Malkele. On tiptoes he can almost

reach her navel. In dreams, he is as tall
as the tower of Babel with might to
confuse the language of cats, birds, pigs, streams.
He weaves her garlands of love-sick flowers,
scents her braids with may-pop, lotus-lilies.
He learns like the mute to perceive a soul
pervade even through the wig (the devil's
face) of a wooden blockhead, learns like the

deaf to hear a glass, emptied of its wine,
weeping like a fiddle, to hear music
of the spheres even through a tin wretch, a
pisspoor pan. Berele Bandoora learns
to map the fate of inanimate worlds.
Junked teakettles begin life anew as
timpani kettledrums, solo street bands,
touch to tears a shell, a bone, a fossil.

Envoy

The dying flame vows to love unto death
the burnt wick as both dwindle into one
tiny firewheel, a speck of nothingness.

Life and death fall, only darkness remains
infinite. Dawn, seraphim land here to
take the village under their three pairs of
wings, fly it to the land of the living.

Marusah

(twin sonnet)

Winter.
Night. Hoarfrost.
The village is
drowned in sleep. Who, if
not Marusah, the sleep
walker would walk out of her
dreams, seeking her lover, hugging
the goblet where wine, vows and blood were
mixed in a toast to their eternal love?
She sees the houses turn into iceborn bears,
the chimneys — snow-eagles, eager to seize, tear their
prey. Led by the moon she walks over the roofs through an
invisible fire which neither life nor death may quench. The
stars (the wise, overworked cliches) are gems out of Satan's crown.

What is left of her lover in this winter-worn village if
not a luring icicle on the eaves of the tranced roof,
(erect as an ice-penis raping a star), which she
licks as a drink offering to love, until it
is a horn of a musk ox piercing her fate,
until she is found — a frozen Venus,
under her unlucky star. Dawn. Clouds:
woolly mammoths carry her like
gold to the devil's treasure;
winds rush to clip their tusks,
to build ivory
castles where she
still dreams, pines.
yearns, loves.

FROM ELCHIK'S LOVE DIARY

In Abandoned Barrack

Dveirke,
Dveirele,
Oi, Dveirinke!
loveliest of bare
foot girls bred on the poor
soil of einkorn wheat, flailed grain,
lilac blue, potato apples.
I write these lines yearning for you in
this abandoned barrack which is stained with
the death of German and red armies who bled
here white; mad with longing, high fever and hounding
whims, left alone to fight fancymongers, a sunset
or two before I die. The winds are here to curse my last
twilights. The late sun is a snowrose in the teeth of the frost.

A Diehard General and You

I see
a diehard
general wave
an alarm flag as
if to incite vengeance
between the conquered and the
victorious dead; and I see
you from the straw roof of a daydream,
a cry's throw through the neighboring time, a
dream or two ago: a flare, a trance from our
queen village; your hair fragrant as a combed field of
flax apt for spinning, your eyes lit with the wisdom of
the ages of Pig Street, our starpaved alley twisted as
the wall-barleys which cleave the murky hovels, to reach the sun.

Still, Clear Night

Stars sleep
on needles
of ice, hushed brooks
are fettered with frost.
Chimney swifts, smoke-blinded,
join the winter moths, flutter
over burnt pentateuchs, seeking
Spring at the last sparks which refuse to
die, scintillate the ashes like rare gems.
Two brave pages (ancient sunsets yellow each
letter) find their way back through the remains of the
synagogue, cover as with the hands of cherubs the
anguished commandment: " thou shalt not kill." Moses leaves
                                            the scorched
tablets, rises wherever the mourned dust is thirsty for tears.

Snowflakes

Outcast
angels who
dared to touch the
earth are born anew
in the arms of snowflakes,
soar in search of God, somewhere
in this bereaved nowhere, until
they melt in their own light leaving here
immortal gloom. The fields are gloried with
the lighthating stars of killed generals, preyed
by the silver eagles which nest in the graves of
colonels. Am I the only one left of old Adam
or did someone bury me long ago and I dream of
you in my grave? I outcry the crows to prove I am alive.

Winter

Winter
is thinning
me into a
lean-jawed wraith, I am
a frightful sight brewed in
hell, could serve as a scare crow.
Archfiends build a castle of ice
besides this desolate barrack to
keep you there as an enchanted princess
yearning for me under a lock of hoarfrost.

Spring

The castle melts into a waterfall, shouting:
Spring is here! Just another thousand years, (between us
and God what is a thousand years?) the streams will rush away
all grief while singing to you, to me, to lucky tomorrows.

Waterfall

Dusk. The
waterfall
at twilight turns
into a sunfall.
Water-girls born in the
waterfall dance in and out
of a rain of gems, (each one is
engraved with your name) laud their only
hour: clasp with water hands to their fate: " Hail!
We will live as long as this sunset," throw their
flowing gowns away, leave their trailing trains to sweep
the day into shadowlands: rise and fall. (Each maiden
with a comb in one hand, a mirror in the other) You
my love, fall the prettiest, fit for the queen of the sunfalls.

Bridemaids

Midnight.
Moonled bride-
maids rush out of
the waterfall, all
ready for our wedding.
Some play on harps of the wind,
some on the choice hues of agate,
opal, jasper, bloodstone, some cascade
water garlands of your fifteen Aprils.
Only you remain chasing the waters to
their beginning before the first stunned tear on earth.
Come O come my love out of the waterfall O just
for an instant, a craving look so that I may live on
forever, Dveirele, a moment or so before I die.

Dveirke's Voice from the Waterfall

Elchik,
Elinke,
for you the light
of my blond braids, the
blossoms of my every
June. O hear the laughter of
the waterfall rout the cries of
the centuries! O leap into the
waterfall, into me, to fall without
a bruise over these hanging cliffs: half lions,
half eagles, griffins guarding the gold of sunsets.
Age in, age out (out of reach of death) scour blood, fear, guts,
humanize the sword, until it may cut the bread of God's
children. The dream, my love, is more real than all realities.

Lowlands

The low
lands are thick
with peat, quagmire,
with the firestink of
decomposing iron
pyrites. Dry rot molds into
one union — friend and foe: rock and
flesh, spear and bone, marrow, pith, bloodroot.
Ghosts of soldiers still battle in the wind.

Dream News

Dream news: Befke parch and Zlatke the blind (thieves,
lovers and tick-beggars) were guests in my dreams, cursed
the guts out of every hoarding skinflint, ground their days
through barrel-organs, broke themselves into pennies and left.
Legless grubs in spongy moor thought they were eagles, rule the skies.

Night Visitor

Itche
the convert
is here. He prays
for the doomed light of
every falling star, points
to the fires of a burning
church, shouting: " I see dawn, dawn, dawn,
born by immaculate conception.
Even the budding graves bulge with pledge, the
melting snows are overflowing with promise."

He went to meet his creator and left me here
to keep vigil over the souls of soldiers, which still
tarry here to share my grief, hurt with every pang of Spring.

Dream News

I saw my dad in America through the seas of longing.

Dawn

The last
darkness of
the night peopled
with specters of dead
soldiers panic against
the first light, moan through every
breeze: " dawn is here!," They are a tale
of woe, run for their lives under the
shrouded eaves where the limpid icicles
hide from Spring, dripping like ornamented tears.

The early bees court the tall buttercups, the fair
maidens of the village. The crocus, the glory of
the snow, the iris, the goddess of the rainbow, coquet
in virgin harems, vie for the bee's sting at the winter's end.

Elchik's Riddles

Dveirke,
what distance
is farther than
you, my love whom I
can not reach? O what is
older than heaven if not
solitude? (Hermit, do not trust
solitude, it can only fondle
its own hoary beard.) If God is older
than solitude what is older than God? If
the dream is older than God what is older than
the dream? Ask the dream, the dream of dumb stone to laugh like
the wind when it carries the stray seeds to join the buds of
tomorrow, the dream of the tree to fly like the eagle, the
dream of the tear to turn into a gem. O ask God, the first
dreamer of you and me: worlds he saw before Genesis.
O then even God was ruled by solitude, praying
to himself for life, for sin. Ask Adam who met
his bride in a dream, falling in love on first
sight, without it no blade of life can grow.
What is younger than this first ray if
not the ray which will rise with the
dawn of tomorrow, O time
gets ever younger; love
dies, hate: immortal
like Azrael,
the angel
of death.

2

How much
darkness is
there in a blind

man's eyes? How much light
in a burning village?
O ask the blind man O ask
the fire. There is as much darkness
in a blind man's eyes as there is light
in our burning village.
How many miles
does a prisoner circle throughout his life
round and round his prison cell? Ask the prisoner,
ask the cell where Eden is seen through a patch of sky.
Only prisoners can count miles beyond time, can measure
years, immeasurable like grief, like the last thoughts of the doomed.

Fugitive

A one
legged, one
eyed soldier limps
through the battleground,
a self accused Cain, a
fugitive from the land of
nod, with a selfmarked forehead: I
am Cain, creator of death of first
murder. He sees the half moon like Abel's
half face white with terror. Gaunt Jews, hollow-cheeked
praying at gleaned vines for abundance run riot,
at the sight of Cain, howling in accord: O vanish
Cain, you caused each field, almshouse, orchard, to bloom with the
                                                          fruit
of beggars' lice. O let the barren earth be mother again!

Gardens of Pig Street

Pig Street:
love-vine, the
virgin's bower,
sprawl, scramble over
the small, red fruit of the
hawthorn; knotweed and spurry,
gasping for breath under the feet
of goats, beggars and birds. Yoorke the
godmaker molds a pale-blue, starving Christ,
for Jesus was suckled on a virgin's milk.
Chatty breezes with seven measures of gossip,
poison themselves as they jabber away the summers
with white snakeroot, sheep laurel, black nightshade. Winged Jews
build at
twilight out of gold — cities of fortune: a flying island.

Harvest...

A field
in harvest
not worth a bean.
The wind garners the
chaff of the grain, the pod
of the pea, the empty glume.

I serenade you my love on
reeds made of straws of oats. Wild roses
bullies of the oldscratch ganglands nip the
harvest in the bud, stab the nurse crop before
yielding grain. Thorn brooms puncture the ears of the corn.
Headache shrubs dissect the heads of the lettuce. Gout flies
invade the barley, the seeds escape in the wind from the
bearded darnels. Grim reapers with hands — scythes,
     reap at dusk the sun.

Seventeen

Dveirke,
I leave for
you all the gold
of my seventeen
autumns, in this year of
nineteen hundred seventeen.

Any living brook will tell you
of my love beyond dust. My witness
here is this tree riddled with bullets, hears
the evil and doom of man as an armless
giant, climbing over this barrack to frighten
the first migrant birds of Spring which swarm around the young
swamps to debate their return southward again. I die with
this prayer: God, dust is sin. O give me flesh — hate made of light.

Beyond

O how
lonely God
will be beyond
the end of time, with
out you and me, without
man, stars and maggots, without
the teeming wonder in your eyes,
without even the grace of death to
elude solitude, to outking omni
present nothingness: doomed to eternity.

Without good and evil, grief and joy, what else will
there be for God to do, if not talk to himself as
I do, facing the lipless mug of Satan, yield only
to his invincible foe, almightier than God — ennui.

Elchik's Last Prayer

God, curse
me not with
the spectered light
of heaven, bless me
with yearning, trance, conflict:
the living darkness of man.
No, not an eternal ghost in
Eden, a bluehearted seraphim,
rather, a stung scorpion on earth, a
wretch under thronged, brotherless feet. Let me not
pray to you with a mouth of dust but with a voice
of drought. Let me cling to the horn of this new moon, to
Satan's teeth, to life. Give me gutterblood, pour
                                    me like waste
waters, free to dream, I am a river sailing to the sea.

Dveirke

Dveirke,
my love, I
see you with the
quaint medallions of
riverbeds, the kinship
of my forefathers, the proud
logmen who swim the beheaded
forests to a new life, resurrect
the little towns, the thatched roofs invite all
birds to build their nests. The hoary trees resurge
into young tables with the scent of old oak or
into barges on the Viliya river; reborn
into woodcraft: arks, fiddles, torchlights. Distances applaud
when we serenade each other on the flutes of hollow reeds.